Order this book online at www.trafford.com
or email orders@trafford.com

Most Trafford titles are also available at major online book retailers.

 www.trafford.com

North America & international
toll-free: 844 688 6899 (USA & Canada)
fax: 812 355 4082

Our mission is to efficiently provide the world's finest, most comprehensive book publishing service, enabling every author to experience success. To find out how to publish your book, your way, and have it available worldwide, visit us online at www.trafford.com

Because of the dynamic nature of the Internet, any web addresses or links contained in this book may have changed since publication and may no longer be valid. The views expressed in this work are solely those of the author and do not necessarily reflect the views of the publisher, and the publisher hereby disclaims any responsibility for them.

Any people depicted in stock imagery provided by Getty Images are models, and such images are being used for illustrative purposes only.
Certain stock imagery © Getty Images.

ISBN: 978-1-4907-3632-7 (sc)

Library of Congress Control Number: 2014909282

Print information available on the last page.

Trafford rev. 07/15/2022

Inward
Expressions

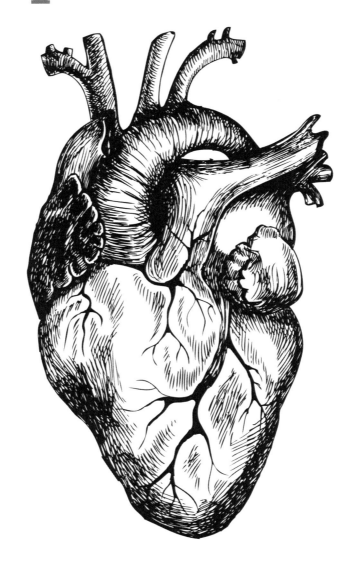

Ronal Reddy

To my friends and family.
Thank you for the support

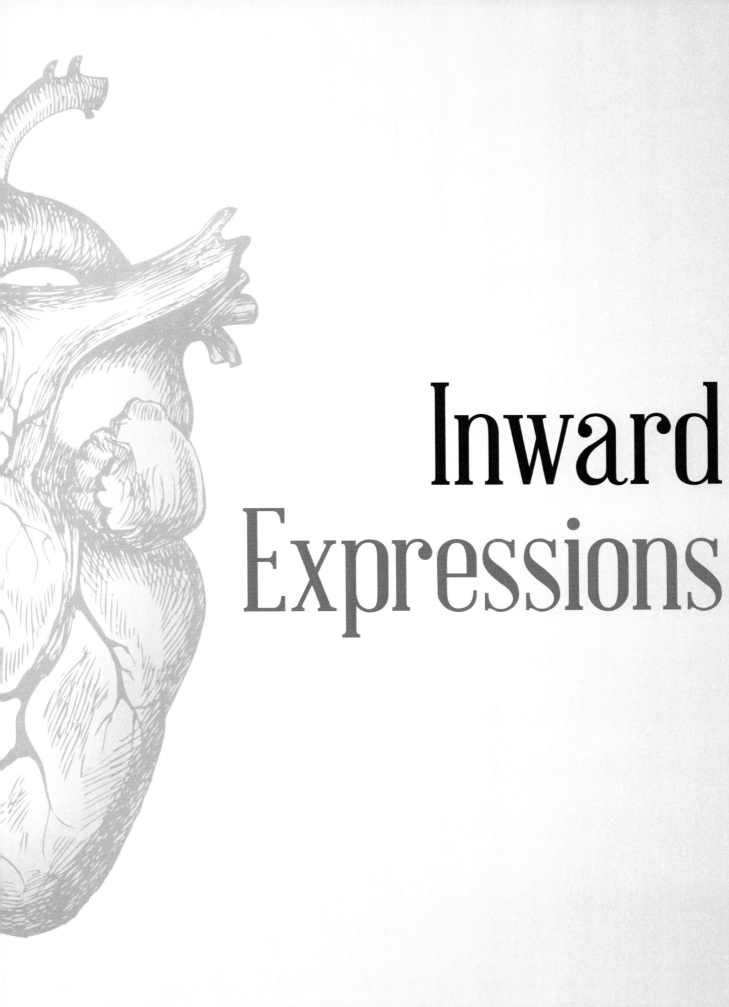

Inward Expressions

Acknowledgements

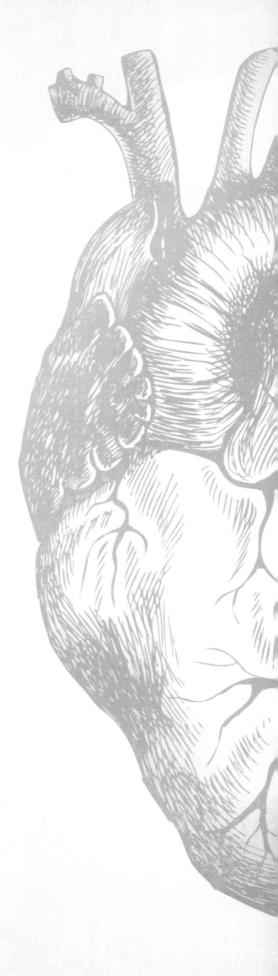

Firstly I would like to thank the Almighty for giving me an opportunity to do something like this.

I would to like to thank my family for believing in me. My friends who thought I could do anything and the people who made this book possible – Trafford Publishing.

A warm thank you to Malcolm Crisp, an English Teacher at Papatoetoe High School who started me off writing poetry.

A world without creativity

Let us examine ourselves

What is something that make us differ?

Differ from others

Differ from their opinions

From their thoughts and attributes

It is the level of creativity.

Creativity, the fulcrum of life

Without it, the world is grey

Dark grey

Creativity is the sun

Shining its rays on us

Boxed, our lives would have been

Shattered our dreams

Creativity as we know it

Would have ceased to gleam.

Death

Life as she knew has gone away

With the Almighty she is to stay

Heavenly life enjoying anew

Memories of her we all shall carry through

For life passes away like a cloud's trace

But memories are immortal, a phase

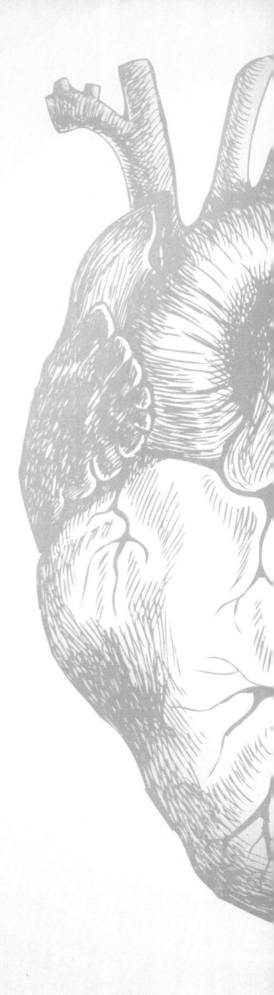

Poetry is . . .

Poetry is the testimony of what is around us.

It is the feeling of peace

A moment of expression

A slice of heaven

It is the way God communicates

A language which means nothing if you lack creativity

Not sophisticated, but sincere

Poetry is emotions

Bundled in words and soaked in all the intangibles

Not perishable, but just made up of different parts

Wintery Train Days

The gloomy dementors have covered the night sky

with cold winds. The winter,

has arrived upon us.

Here I am, sitting in a train.

From Britomart to Manukau.

'Stopping at all stations' says the cold automated voice.

The train stops, the conductor blows the whistle

and away it goes. To a different station.

I hear the sounds of the engine roaring.

The wheels turning, as it strikes against the iron rails

The sun has gone to bed, tucked in by the clouds

The moon has not yet greeted the night sky.

Just clouds. Dark grey clouds

Invading the wintery night sky

Giving clues of tomorrow's outcome.

Winter

I stood there shadowing the happening:

The clouds, like lurking demons,

About to strike like predators;

Fields, streets covered in a white blanket.

Casting my vision upon the lakes to find

A glass coffin . . . trapping water

In quest of the noisy shadows beside the stream

Where branches are thrown over the pool

Branches swaying from side to side hence in the windy frozen wasteland

Rocks beside the brook paved with coldness.

Looking up I see birds in a V formation,

Smoke like an outstretched arm reaching for the sky,

Contaminating the air

With gloom and despair.

Time

It takes no sides and has no enemies because it is just.

Time.

Has no

friends and still

hangs around with all.

A river rushing reluctantly rigorously,

time has no time to waste.

Time is money some say, but never

understand what they mean by this wonderful saying.

Methods of time have changed but time itself has

stayed the same. A little sleep and folding of hands

and poverty hunts you down. Look at the ants, the creation

of God. They have no chief or king, yet they work persistently.

In Time they are able to gather according to what they will need

and enough to last the whole winter season. Learn from them

We must.

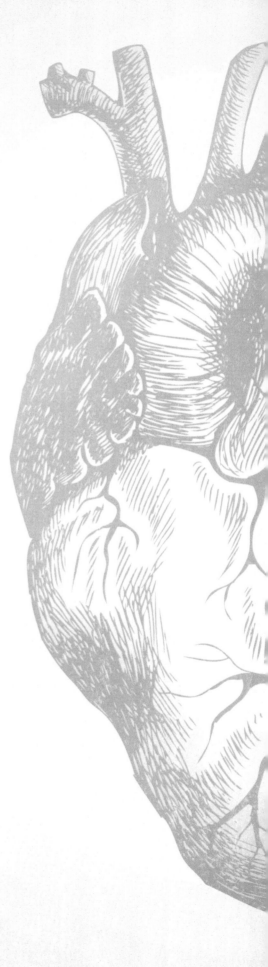

Death

What a sensation!
The curtains are drawn and the show has finished.
However, there is no audience. No applause.
Life as you know it has ended.
The bright, sunshine-filled day
Is now a dark, silent graveyard.
That this flesh should perish quite,
And all of life's spring cease to flow.

Thoughts cease, and immortality no longer
Lingers in the mind lying in silence.
The sands of time will not flow back.

As it lies in the silent grave,
Howling winds over the carcass,
Nothing is heard of or done
As it is wrapped in the ropes of flora.

Dear Friend, From France

Encapsulated in a wooden

chrysalis by incommunicable depression,

writing to you my first letter.

Dying to listen to a "How are you?"

like a wilted rose I have ceased to bloom.

Like a starving animal I have decayed vigorously.

Moments of delight have perished.

Beaune has shown my past; how

I sat and stared at the Yonne River.

I am ever so unapparent now that

I can hide my emotions.

My mind is empty, but

thoughts provokingly question my anxiousness.

I can return to you and

let my friendship be known.

Yet this abyss cannot be bridged.

Love

Your Friend

From Paris

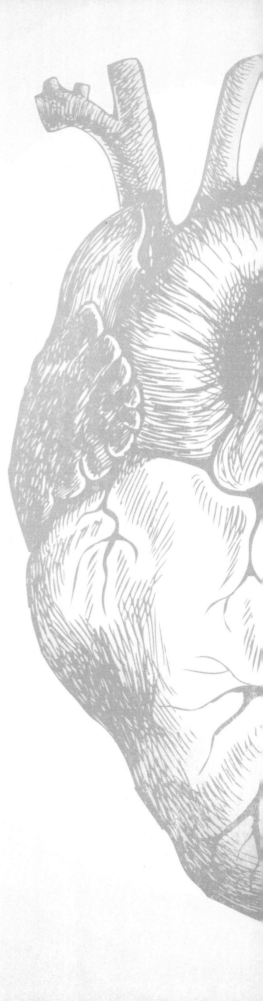

Who am I?

The gusty, jagged blow upon the mast,

Gratis howls of the raging oceans

Creating spectacles of soldiers

Of the times of 87 B.C.

Funderfully, enchanted sediment, Selah!

Like dew in early morning grass,

Mild resentment of the savoury aroma

Grousing shrill between fissure in crags

To a placid breeze upon the face of land.

What am I?

Wind

Your heart is—

Different and unusual,

Jittery and jolly,

Willing and can.

Prepared and dominant,

Alive and well,

Peaceful and in harmony.

Filled with drama.

Weak at times and

Strong at other times.

Skipping beats and

Occupying the blood.

Jam-packed with ideas.

Fresh as lettuce.

Aspiring with ambition,

Greasy with knowledge,

Uncivilized as pigs.

Without a leash.

Captures an inhumane emotion – love.

But most of all it needs fortification,

For out of it flow the issues of life.

Forgiven

What can't be lived with
Should be forgiven.
What is often forgiven
Should be forgotten.
What can't be forgotten
Should be given away to someone who can.

When I needed help

When I needed help I went to my parents.

I knew they knew that they were smarter.

But they told me to go to the teachers.

So I went to the teachers.

I knew they knew that they were smarter.

But they told me to go to the priests.

So I went to the priests.

I knew they knew that they were smarter.

But they told me to go to God.

So I went to God.

I knew that he knew that he was smarter.

He said, "Where's your faith?"

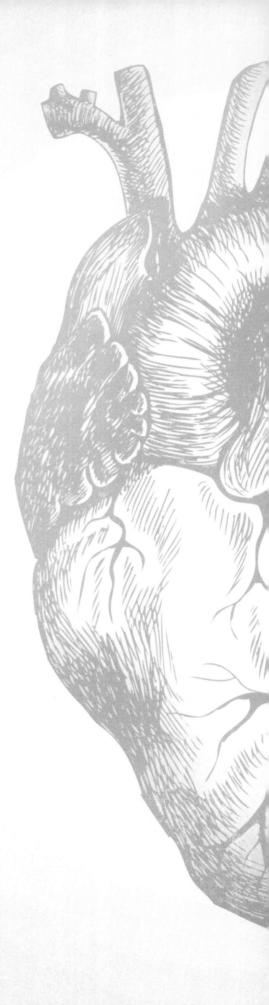

Life is . . .

Life is like a bowl of steamed rice:
You eat it while it's hot, or else there is no special taste to it.

Life is like a salmon:
You try to jump through the current, and you make it,
But it's no use because you get eaten by the bear.

Life is like a tree planted by the river side:
As long as there is water, the tree stands.

Life is like a computer:
You must keep saving your work, or else it will be lost forever once it shuts down.

Life is like a mirror:
It only shows you what it wants to show you and not what you want to see.

Life is like a dark room where you have to find the light switch in order to see.

A child

Born out of seeds.

Different seeds.

An innocent bud, opening in the world.

Not knowing of existing devouring beasts.

Born of a pure heart,

With original sin.

Born with a new perspective,

A new dream, desire

Slowly sprouting into maturity,

But suddenly creeping along notorious norms.

And gone!

A child no more.

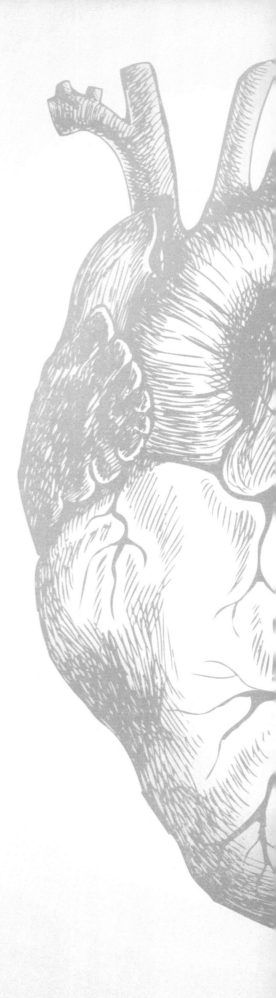

Love is Patient

Ah – the physics of love!
Love is patient,
Kind, envies no one.

Love bears all things
Magnetic.

The salmon that swims,
swims to get to you –
Only in the process
to be devoured by distrust.

It breaks me
To let you go. Patience is hard work.
I envy patience –
A sin, you may call it,
but the truth.

A dark gloomy day

Yesterday the sky spoke to me.

It told me that tomorrow he was going to cry.

I asked him why?

He didn't reply.

The next day it rained.

It started with some slow showers.

And it grew and grew

Until large droplets of water

Filled the pot holes on the road.

He cried and he cried and he cried

Each drop I saw, showed me his pain.

But I couldn't do anything

Everyone whined when he cried.

But no one knew why the sky would cry.

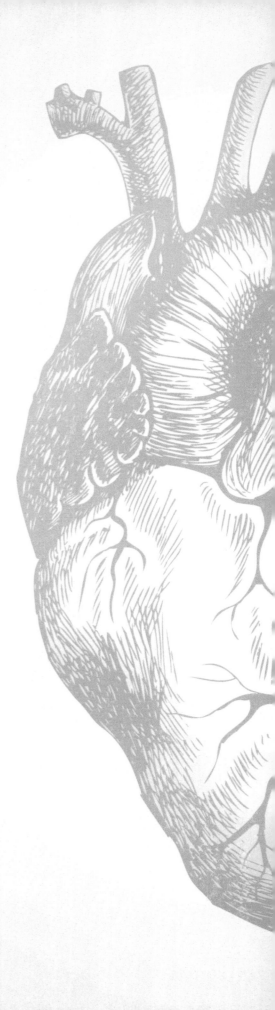

The little girl

I saw a little girl
Selling papayas by the side of the road.
She was a sweet little girl
She sold papayas every day.

I met her once and introduced myself
She told me her name was Lucy
I asked her where she lived.
She told me under the bridge

Lucy told me about her parents
How they had died
Now, she is all alone
Selling papayas by the side of the road.

The missing tree

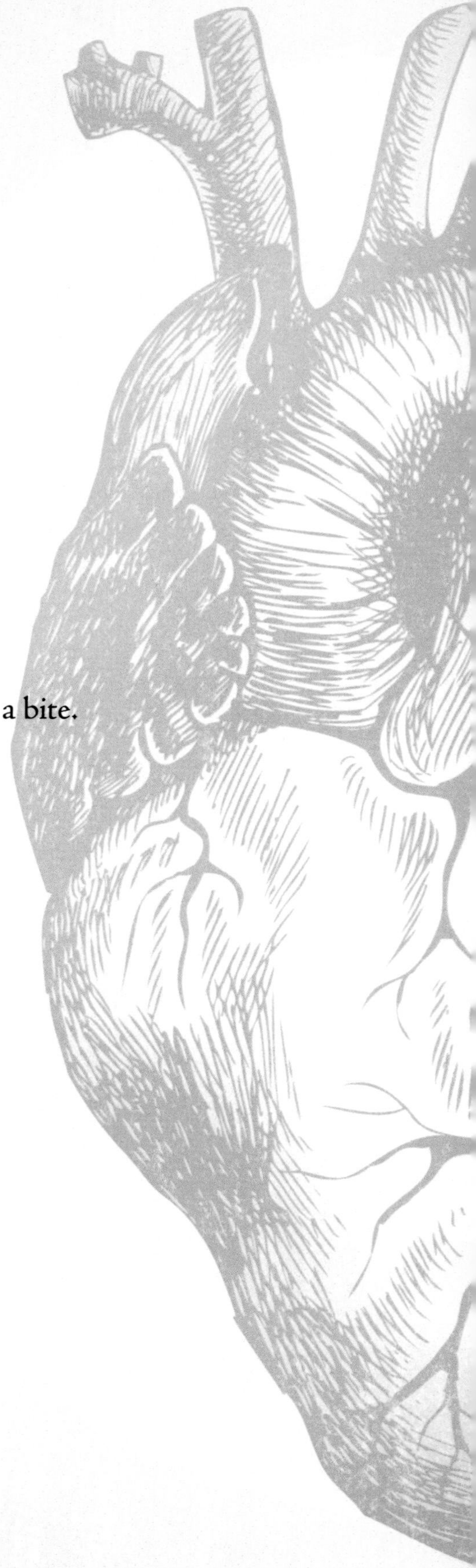

There is mum, dad, me, little brother Bill and little sister Anna
There is everyone,
but the Nectarine tree is missing in the photo.
It was always there when I was young.
I dream about it always.
Its sweetness.
Its smoothness.
The stories about dad he reminded me of.
And the nectarine juice that dribbled out my mouth when I took a bite.
It's gone now.
Never to be seen again.
Just a memory, forever
To be shared.
I could meet Him again
But death, would have to be my best friend.

Old photographs

Today was my grandmother's birthday
She took out her golden bejeweled box
Full of her treasures.
Her moist burgundy colored lipstick
Her necklace,
And an old photograph of my grandparents

They looked happy
Through the stained, old, dog eared photograph.
I saw the photo
But she saw through it
Her day, filled with laughter
The picture came to life
It captured their likeness,
Their memories
The photograph is a bridge for her through her lonely abyss,
Into Her world.
Which she found in her golden bejeweled box
Full of her treasures.

The broken heart

A broken heart can rarely be mended.

Cannot be stitched together

And cannot be glued easily.

A page washed along the banks

Cannot be retrieved of the information it once showed,

Only time could turn the tides, which it won't.

Trust is the remedy which is bought without money.

Dear is the cost yet shows no loss,

Only profits, up.

And therefore a heart broken no more.

Sewn together with the,

Thread of trust.

Educated or Influenced?

There I sat in the church.

Listening, to the preacher as he

Linked all his words to God.

He is talking, about

The creator and the creation

The Risen Lamb

The Prince of Peace

The King of Jews.

But by all this,

Am I to be educated or influenced?

Dreams

I want to go to France and see such

A majestic tower, sitting on its own.

Absorb the vibe and return with a thrill of exuberant experience.

I want to sit and enjoy a pizza or spaghetti and meatballs

In an Italian restaurant in Italy,

Listening to Nessun Dorma!

I want to soar the mirrored sea:

The excitement of leaving the ground with a roar,

And landing with the joy of having felt the blades cut through the air.

I want to open the eyes of my exploration and

Discover the heart of the Amazonian jungle –

To unravel the secrets of nature –

Search with a found heart,

Think without thinking,

Dream without doubting.

Blossom

Flowers yawn in their slumber,
Trees shake their arms to rid of strains,
River starts to race at normal pace,
And the ground blossoms new grass.

It is this scene we adore
The splendor of spring comes forth
Spreading the pollen of freshness,
Filling with wonder and beauty.

The sensation of peace and quietness,
Robins and bluebirds singing as they nourish their children
Sunshine beaming from above, piercing the leaves
Reflecting on the dew fresh on the grass.

The heaven's firmament is clear blue,
With not a single sign of a cloud.
Birds soaring in the air, animals awakening,
Each emigrating to their pride.

Feeling the air so pure and fragrant,
Fruits unravel the flavor of the season
By the gleam of the morning cinders
Blossom has blossomed.

Love?

I remember the days just like yesterday

When it all happened

Like two swans

We shall never depart he told me

For better or for worse he told me

But here I am

Alone in my worse times

Without the vowed man

My first child he told me

Would be named after him

But when the time came for his arrival

My 'husband' just left

In sickness and in health he told me

He would be there

But when I became ill

He disappeared

I live alone now

Without my 'husband'

When people ask me of my true love

I ask them, 'What love?'

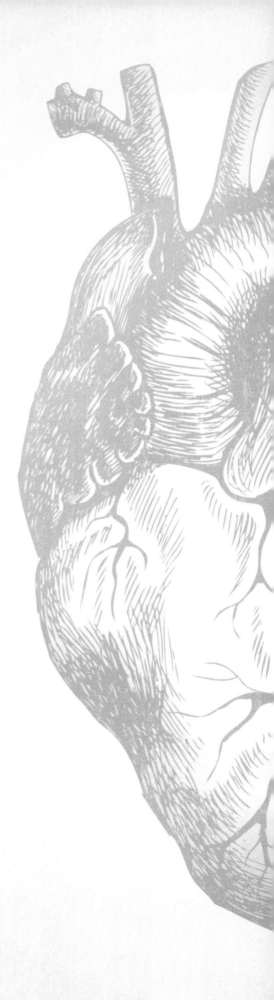

Night beauty

The moon portrays the beauty of the night,
The waters below charm the pohutukawa next to them
To sway from side to side to the voodoo of the wind,
Instructing moths to dangle in moonlight galore.

The owl hooting in the moonlight, creating
Lovely night rhythm filled with mystery;
Mountains creating spooky distraction,
Howling the fiction of the night.

Flowers prefer to smooch the ground
Than stand with pride in the malicious night;
Breaking the silence of the hour
Pops out a creature of utter annoyance.

The night stays pure and still
Until the shadows of the sun pull out their swords
To strike against the dark,
The rays invade the dark and declare: Retreat!

Autumn

Oh splendid autumn!
Ooze out your beauty,
Like mist upon placid morn,
Like waves upon sandy beaches.

Bewilder a giddy peace
Upon the vain earth,
Allowing the sun to cast its final rays
Without cease.

Night falls and the chilled air creeps in between,
Sending a frisson down the spinal cord of nearby lakes
To presage the arrival of the arctic –
Oh, why must the autumn bring about cold?

The sun hides its face when the clock strikes six;
Visualize the lurking of winds, cold winds.
Leaves whisper the sounds of our history;
Beauty grows weak, covered in snow it withers.

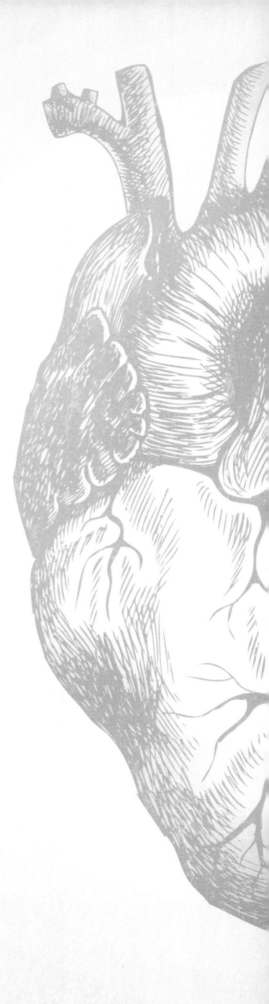

What is love?

Is it a word without zest; or a labyrinth, or a lacerating emotion?

Simply deep affection or fondness for each other.

Love feels like trampling on morning dew

On the lush green grass

With our naked feet,

Feeling the emotion cast out

Like waves soaked at the margins of the sea.

Looks like a sprinting cheetah

Hunting with an exhilarated heart;

Smells like roses cross-pollinated with violet flowers

From the courts of Aphrodite herself.

Tastes like sweet honey

Marvelously derived from the beehive;

Sounds like jingling church bells,

Filling every moment with adoration.

Winter

Cold, damp

Freezing, cooling, shivering

Soup, apple pie, ice-cream, sun-screen lotion

Tanning, hydrating, swimming

Sunny, humid

Summer

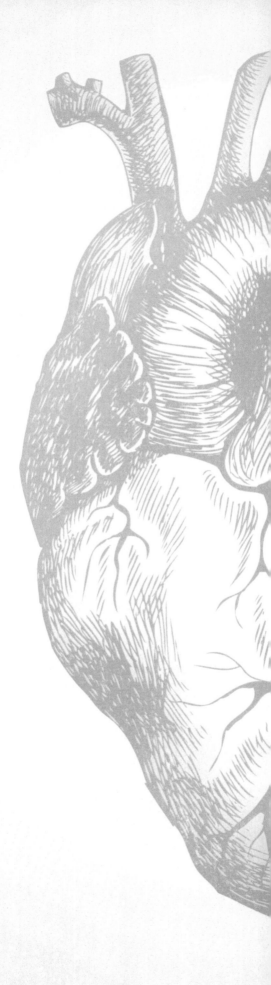

A season?

Love to me is just a season
Each comes with its terms
Seldom does it stay to please
Often it fades and goes

Hard to catch and difficult to brew
Yet the strongest taste I would ever know
For it is like a barking dog
Which seldom lays a bite

Stencils of love many have produced
To implement their marks
But a few are real gold
Bite and see, to know if it was worth the sold

My love

Each day I would dream about her

So beautiful she was

She was ever so opulent

So bright, cheerful and flowery

Luscious and soft was her touch

Goosebumps were discovered on my arms

I never lusted for no one

Midori, she was called

In the morning she filled me with warm energy

And at night her cool charms put me to bed

But she was dying

Each day she talked about how she was treated

I listened, but nothing I could do

For part of her death I was, somehow

The Morning

The dark world

Waiting for a light

Where is the light going to come from?

Who will give out the light?

Suddenly peaking from the horizon

Emerges a light. A semicircle of rays

Bringing about warmth to fauna and flora

Let the heavens open and shout,

Out the morning

Let the moon move aside and

Escort the sun – Savior of the day to rule over

Bluebirds and Robins tweeting about

Preaching the arrival of the chosen one

'Make way, make way. For it is here'

Visiting my Grandmother

I liked visiting my grandma

She taught me lessons

She taught me about people

She showed me how I was before

And how I am now

Grandmother was always there

Each step of the way she helped me

When I thought of her

Problems would find a way

And fear would run away

It was like time travelling

The best experience ever

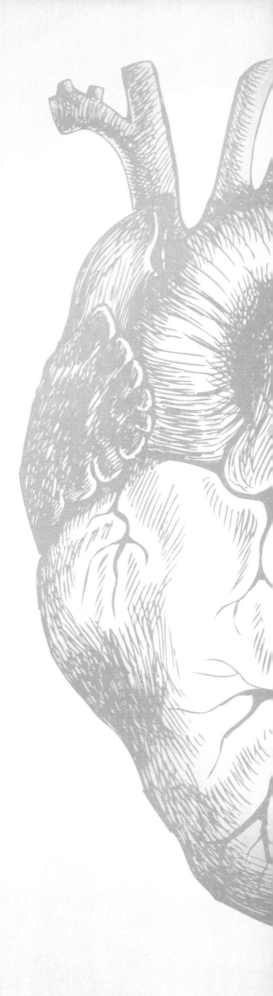

The Airport

The airport, I work in
A house of destinations
A lot come through as visitors
But a few fly off as passengers

Where do they go?
Why do they go?
Maybe where they were yet
Had some minor glitches

Golden particles, the pillars are made off?
Roof as high as the sky?
Gates impregnable like the Fort Knox?
Yet the road in is as thin as a thread?

Why go to a place where it is so expensive to stay,
No privacy whatsoever,
Highly monitored and secured,
And not a lot of room to pass through?

Our Society

The world is just as complex as the human eye

It moves very differently

It sparks charisma in my heart

A feeling of pure divinity

Different things separate me from this world

Feelings and emotions that are Real

Questioning thoughts is the

Definition of culture – the way of life

It repels from our thinking often

But it may hold a very surprised message

Maybe sung by the trees, or hummed by the bees

It still comes from the world we know it

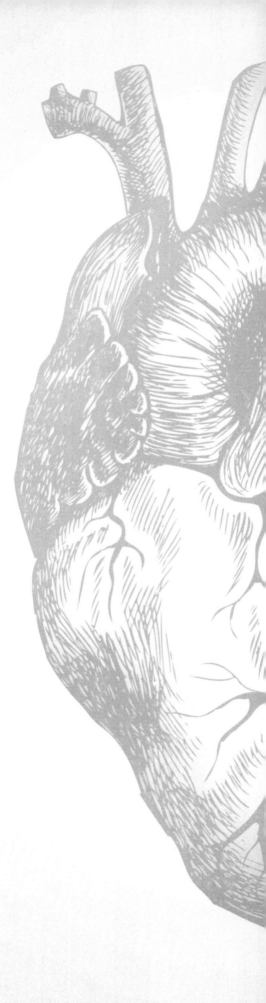

Wedding

The lovely bonds of nature
Bring about happiness and lavish accordance
Of pure divinity in the midst of audience

With joy and acceptance, a wedding is designed
To give peace of heart and mind
Jingling bells and cheers of happiness
Speak of the moment of love

Violins, bass and oboe
Playing melodious music to grasp this
Special moment of delight
A feeling of love not known of

Those times, memories we have spent together
Cord to cord, mail to mail
You were far from me, yet it felt real close
A great bond of love exposed today
In front of you all it lay

Change

Change is the equilibrium of belief

A fuel injector for a rising civilization

Change could be good, or bad

However, choice of change is essential

Change is not about the future

It is about now

It is a matter of acceptance

Change is not institutional, but an evolution

Change is the splitting of a testa and

Emerging of a radicle – a process some would call it

Change varies like species

A search, because what found is always treasure

Choice

A choice is an act of decision

Helpless consistency or tedious objection

Imagine the best of nature aiming at you

Entrepreneurs of the land

Since the Garden of Eden

Live like a beggar on the streets

Or an entrepreneur of the land

Think of new and genuine ideas

To escape the danger of bondage

By thinking of the situation

For new innovative ideas

You envisage a new land

Where one of your own decisions determines your future

Good Afternoon

I sat there on the park bench,
Under the willow swinging and swaying branches
The sun smiled at the chirping birds
And beamed its rays on the creek nearby

As the grass curled itself into shape
To be painted with dew in the morning
Flowers looking at each other and nodding in the wind
Giving their final goodbye's for the day

The query bees in a swarm
Invaders of the privacy of the flowers
Heading back to their beehive
With pride and ending their day of strive

The fish in the creek blowing bubbles of dismay
At the dawning of the sun

Children tired of play in the breeze
Decide to go home for the day
Leaving the park all alone
As it was found yesterday

Now you see the sun going down
Like being dunked into a giant cup of tea
Smiling the welcome of Lunar
To shine in its own beauty

Upendi

Arm in arm you have protected me

With your strength through the roots

You have shown me the conduit towards prosperity

And the field of memories I see ahead

Eyes glued to each other, abbreviates the association

Of two love saplings reaching for the sky

And out of their adolescent chrysalis

To find the firmament of realism

Such is the influence of love

Tantalizing the first savor of Upendi

Time

Time is like the waves of an ocean
Bringing in fresh fish on the shore or
Destruction through some?

Perhaps this is the undertake of special tides
Where the current brings new beginnings

Time and tide waits for no man
May not be so true
For man is the purpose
Of the existence of time and tide

The lost city

Roads paved with gold
Lampposts shimmering like silver

The gentle sound of the waterfall
Creating a lullaby
Rocks nearby, bejeweled
Fish, like swimming diamonds

The garden of beauty
Filled with fragrance of flowers, not present in any perfume
The color of it is so profound
The touch of it so divine

Oozing beauty and refreshment
Amazing grace how sweet the sight
Seemed so diligent in the light of day
And shimmering in Lunar's ray

Is there such a city that I talk of?
Happening without the knowledge of this world

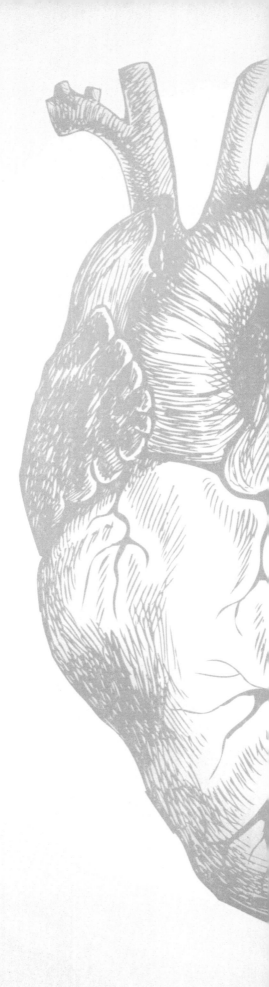

Where there are streets paved with gold, if you want it to

Where such beauty exists, if you want it to

It is place you can steal from, and never get caught

A place where adolescence is the only life

Where money doesn't matter, and work is inoperable

A place we can only describe but not provide

What is Life?

Is it the capacity for growth? Or perhaps continual change until death

However you define it, it still does not change the fact

That our lives are not really our lives

We mimic what we see

Is it because of a feeling of belonging, or self-satisfying?

We do not know.

We tend to be carried away by the current like a fish losing its directions

Life's boat is very immense to go through the cave of discontent

Why be so down and gloomy?

Take a moment to look beyond the horizon

Past the cloud of sadness and look at the ray of happiness

But take time to look back, and see life smiling back at you.

Aspirations

Floating without a care of tomorrow

Are cottons in the sky

Sometimes squeezing out,

Or not visible.

The sunshine brings his cottony friend with him,

But in the night it often disappears.

I lay back and watch these aspirations,

And imagine giant white fluffy bunnies

Hopping about in the cloudy garden.

If I could just reach out and touch them

I would be complete.

They travel, yes they do!

But where they go, nobody knows.

Birthday

A birthday.

Time for a celebration,

Time to remember your birth.

A time to remember that you are maturing.

Adolescent has expired and retirement is to knock your door.

But above all,

It's the heart, which needed not expire,

For age is not what a birthday celebrates,

But the joy of being alive.

Experiencing life.

And making you remember your time on this planet,

Has been worthwhile?

What is hate?

A strong word some would say

Is it a word with zest; or not a labyrinth?

Simply no affection or fondness for anything

Hate feels like trampling on compost with our naked feet

A hollow feeling

Like an angry dog with rabies

Looks like a wilted rose

Without emotions

Smells like mouldy cheese

Only to be devoured my untamed rats

Taste like bitter coffee

Marvelously derived from beans

Sounds like an annoying whining adult

Filling every moment with disappointment

Modern poetry

It was yesterday,

I remember picking up the quill

To write a sonnet

To craft a living piece of art.

Poetry was the way, of articulation

An awe inspiring truth

A vigilant skill, tied in one knot

It was a feeling, a good feeling

A few complications

But still understandable

Now poetry has a new face,

An improved face

People understand it

People articulate with it

We reason for it

But whatever the style

Maybe, the feeling of it all

Will not change entirely.

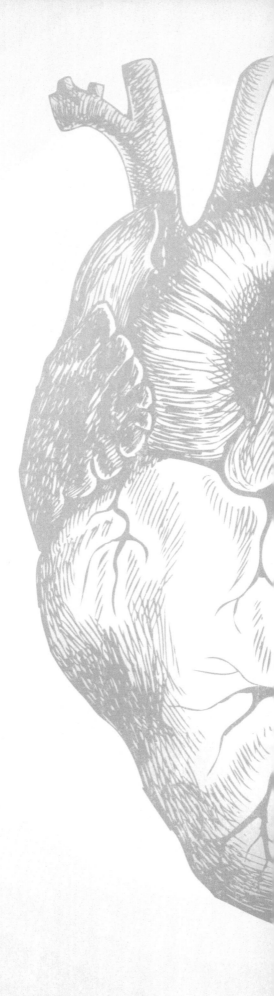

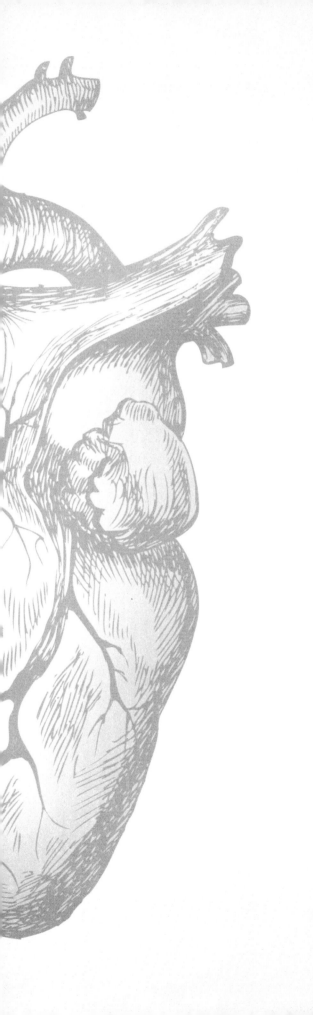

Printed in the United States
by Baker & Taylor Publisher Services